A VOICE COMING
FROM THEN

//

JEREMY DIXON

*EMILY
GREAT TO
MEET YOU +
GOOD LUCK WITH
THE NEW BOOK!
JEREMY
10/21*

ARACHNE PRESS

First published in UK 2021 by Arachne Press Limited
100 Grierson Road, London, SE23 1NX
www.arachnepress.com

© Jeremy Dixon 2021

ISBNs
Print: 978-1-913665-40-1
ePub: 978-1-913665-41-8
Mobi/Kindle: 978-1-913665-42-5
Audio: 978-1-913665-43-2

Printed on wood-free paper in the UK by TJ Books, Padstow.

Thanks to Muireann Grealy for her proofreading.

Cover design: Rachel Marsh of Semple Press.

CONTENT WARNING

Some poems in this book deal with themes
and expressions of physical and verbal bullying,
swearing, homophobia, homophobic language,
queerphobia, attempted suicide and suicide.

// a note on content warnings

For me content warnings really work. If I am not
prepared then sometimes just seeing the word
suicide has an emotional effect. The poems do not
go into graphic detail but some of them do include
the themes mentioned above. Please feel free not to
read any further or to come back later if, or when,
you are ready.

// a note on the use of the word queer

Queer is a word loaded with emotional and historical
meanings, some people see it as a slur, others reclaim
it as a source of pride. I use it in this book to identify
those who exist outside of heterosexualism and to
embrace wider ideas of strangeness, inclusivity,
activism and acceptance.

// a note on the use of italic text

Using italic text in the body of a poem indicates that
those words have been quoted from another person
or from a book, diary, letter, interview or social
media post.

for he who lives more lives than one
more deaths than one must die
Oscar Wilde
The Ballad of Reading Gaol

dedicated to Wednesday 13 June 1979
and to all those who we have lost
and to those who remain
and to my family

CONTENTS

INTRODUCTION

On Wednesday 13 June 1979, three months after my 15th birthday, I waited until dad drove mum into Cardiff for her night shift as a Staff Nurse then went into the kitchen and stole the paracetamol tablets she stored under the sink. After taking them I fell asleep on the sofa in my bedroom. I woke up suddenly at about 2am and proceeded to vomit for the next six hours, which is probably why I am still alive today.

This is the note that at the time I didn't understand myself enough to write...

IN CHESTER WITH MY SISTER TWO MONTHS BEFORE

IN SOUTHEND WITH MY GRANDMOTHER TWO MONTHS AFTER

casting the runes with Spring-Heeled Jack

we are here from the future
we are here in the past

our demon fingers
scraping out your throat

where pills still taste the same
still absorb your teenage spit

so even when you can't
remember your body

be grateful for the gallbladder
that your gut can still pulse

be grateful for a liver
strong enough to cope

be grateful for our gag reflex
for the stomach that overruled

this is a binding
to keep us safe

wraiths

so this is a poem where I meet Anne Sexton
when I am three years old and lost

I am three years old and lost and she grabs me
in the foyer of the Royal Festival Hall in London

Anne Sexton grabbing me when I run away
from my mother in the foyer of the Royal Festival Hall

and I run straight into the sheer legs of Anne Sexton
talking to men a circle of men around her I run

straight into her legs and she laughs
drops down level with my face and laughs

picks me up and swings me on her hips
swaying on Anne Sexton's hips as she strides

the foyer of the Royal Festival Hall looking
for a mother and recognising my mother

by reading the fear in an unfamiliar face
reads my mother handing me over with a smile

a smile and the slightest tap on my mother's stomach
her tapping and saying *Let's hope this one's a girl*

a girl and a slight tap and a cigarette walking away
Anne Sexton walking back to the men and my mother

staring and recognising that smile on a spotlit poster
a poster for poetry in the foyer of the Royal Festival Hall

so this is a poem where I meet Anne Sexton in London
when I am three years old when we are both unmourned

Sunday School

we are taught to make Tabernacles
and miniature Arks of the Covenant

from worksheets and cocktail sticks
speared into polystyrene ceiling tiles

we are taught to hate Judas
because he kissed Jesus

betraying him for
short-term financial gain

we must also despise Judas
for the sin of self-murder

swinging from *Cercis siliquastrum*
the white flowers

turning red with blood
and shame

before the motorway

you're making a home
of the suicide tree

a hole in the roots
the size of a child

to slither through
its moss interior

wide enough
for small arms

at full stretch
to push against

this wooden funnel
open to the sky

and the twisted branches
where once they'd found

something rotting
something hung

the friendly

dad shouts from the boundary
he wants his white jumper

from the long leather bag
in the changing rooms *now*

you will always hate cricket
so you dog-ear the Famous Five

slouch to the splintered pavilion
navigating slatted benches

clothes on pegs wet towels
steam Brut and cigarettes

the showers turn off
and a tall man walks out

wet hair naked dripping
wicket keeper thighs

he sees you and smiles
rubbing himself dry

what the hell took you so long
sorry daddy I got a bit lost

dear Jack

it is very late and I can hear chains
being dragged along the lane

outside my bedroom window
is it you doing that

if it is then please stop
because I can't sleep

you know I have school tomorrow
and I'm terrified

I don't think
I will make it to 16

PS
mum says I should ignore you

that you will get bored
leave me alone

in the past 12 months 25% of young people
in the UK experienced bullying

//

in the past 12 months 40% of LGBTQ+ young people
seriously considered attempting suicide

while more than 50% of transgender
and non-binary youth seriously considered

Annual Bullying Survey, Ditch The Label, 2020

National Survey on LGBTQ Youth Mental Health,
The Trevor Project, 2020

last three months in England

5 January 1977: *first day back at school. When I came home I found my piano report. I passed by one point.*

7 January: *in Biology we used plasticine to make animals. I made a giraffe. But PP broke the neck off.*

8 January: *the washing machine overflowed and flooded the entire kitchen. We watched Doctor Who.*

10 January: *in the small game I scored a try. Dad had a minor accident and smashed the car.*

13 January: *it was the worst blizzard in this country for 14 years. The school bus came at 4.32pm.*

18 January: *in French SE tipped over our desk and all of us were sent out. Mr Y said he'd use the cane.*

19 January: *a pair of boots went missing (stolen). Police were called to the school to find out who did it.*

9 February: *in Woolworths in Cardiff a lady truant officer stopped us to ask why we weren't at school.*

14 February: *in Badminton I won 3 games out of 4. On the bus home I was pestered by PP and SE.*

16 February: *in the morning I felt sick and had diarrhoea. A dog ran away after being hit by a car.*

20 February: *went to Sunday School. T and I nicked sweets from the coffee bar. Hope no one finds out.*

28 February: *went to school. Had a brilliant game of rugby. RH nearly broke my arm. Had my bath early.*

2 March: *missed the school bus because I stayed a bit too long at Drama club. Mr S gave me a lift home.*

7 March: *Dad went up to Cardiff early in the morning. I was one of the killers in killer wink.*

15 March: *M came back today after the bin business. Played scrabble in Mr H's office. Had a German test.*

16 March: *played in Mr H's office at break and dinner, our own private club! Went to Drama club.*

17 March: *in basketball PP, SE and RH tried it on, so mum rang up the school. Seeing Mr C tomorrow.*

18 March: *went to Mr C and told him about PP, SE and RH. They were all told off. Went to Stamp club.*

21 March: *went into Mr H's office. Had an early lunch. Played the piano. Watched Charlie's Angels.*

25 March: *did Human Biology. Went to Mr H's office. Janet stayed off school because she was ill.*

27 March: *last time at Sunday School. Mum received two plants and a card. Mrs T sang, 'What a friend…'*

29 March: *2X had collected money for a going-away present. It was a Papermate. I had to give a speech.*

30 March: *moved to Wales today. The Pickfords van came at 10.15am. Tom ran away but we caught her.*

in the back with Spring-Heeled Jack

spring-time Jubilee year
the day of relocation

we're stretched across the rear seat
of their Hillman Hunter parked

outside The Angel hotel
refusing to move

however much they shout
or try to persuade

for three locked hours
we lie low from passersby

constructing a fragile safety
in an unfamiliar place

knowing our voice will betray us
in the difference of each first hello

we can foresee the head-butts
the pushes into nettles

every blast of warm spit
that will slide down our cheek

buddies

you're playing choke games
at lunchtime

holding your breath
with Tim behind

hugging your chest
until you slump to the floor

someone says
your mouth was twitching

the one out longest
should be unbeatable

we surround you at the top
of the Quad's concrete steps

the safety of home
one push away

bless you hay fever

for the snot the sneezes
the red raw nostrils

the sprays across maths books
the blots smudging essays

the no keeping it in
the not going out

of being excused
the battleground fields

during every recess
to be sheltered from

those angry ones
we now praise

for every taunt pinch and slap
for knowing so much sooner than we did

exalting those shadows
we grow through

that with time we learn
not to give as good as we got

that our allergic response
is how we survive

sidelines

men
terrify me

what they
shout

what
they chew

how they
spit

every petty
alliance

kicking
into touch

those motherfucking
hugs

Trojans

the gift of an enemy is no gift and brings no good

Ajax the Great
fell on his own sword

hilt down
blade up

the sword that once
was Hector's sword

exchanged for his own red belt
after they went at it

hammer and tongs
all day long

he said *I'll be your friend*
if you swear you're not queer

HATE THAT NICK NAME

Jeremy

the name itself carries a whiff of lily-livered mummy's boy

it begins with	*Oi! Dickinson!*
unwanted contraction	*Dickinson you ponce!*
a short leap from *Jezzer*	to running scared
to *Jerry*	through arcades
to *Jez*	to coming round
then *Jay*	on Victorian slabs
to *J*	jumping from *sensitive*
rhymes with Gay	to *too sensitive*
from *seems like*	to *woke*
a nice boy	to *weirdo*
to *bum boy*	to *bent*
to *Jeremy Thorpe*	to *fag*
to *Quentin*	to *queer*
to *poofter* to	*don't bleed on me*

Paracetamol is the most common drug
taken in overdose in the UK

each year about 100,000 people present to emergency
departments with paracetamol poisoning

//

people vary in susceptibility
to paracetamol

many people who overdose appear to recover
then a few days later develop fatal liver failure

The 2nd Atlas of Variation in Risk Factors
and Healthcare for Liver Disease,
Public Health England, 2017

Report in Which? – The Consumers' Association, 1994

13 June 1979 with Spring-Heeled Jack

I decide to die in my bedroom watching
BBC WALES in black and white

seven forty-five
ASK THE FAMILY gulp

eight ten new drama
a series in 10 parts

THE ΩMEGA FACTOR swallow
Episode One: The Undiscovered Country

mmm James Hazeldine Leela
still swallowing

an evil bookshop
psychic Felo-de-se empty

THENINEOCLOCKNEWS
with/Angel/aRip/pon

t h e   s c r e e n   i s   f a d i n g
you've made it // ALL STOP

for you...

—

Oi! Jeremiah!
only the living turn pages

the recidivist

you spew orange bile
into a cardboard bowl

while your ward neighbour
in biker leathers convulses

strapped to their bed
both sides up

they scream
please let me die

you dream of motorbikes
and decapitations

when you awake
their cubicle is empty

and you didn't dare ask
and you still don't know

numbers

doctors queried
just how many

I had counted
down exactly

between gulps of
orange juice

planning to leave
in the slow change

between Wednesday
and Thursday

between mum's night shift
and dad waking to pick her up

instead I begin to puke
sometimes the universe sways

allows a
recalculation

a consultant child psychiatrist's letter
to a hospital doctor dated 20 June 1979
which I first read forty years later

I interviewed your patient
on Ward West 5 on 15 June 1979

and also spoke
with his parents

Jeremy took an overdose
of paracetamol tablets

following certain
school stresses

ie following
bullying

there were no evidences
that the domestic situation

has produced
an intolerable situation

or indeed there was anything
other than a good relationship

between this adult
and his parents

quite why he went
so far on account

of school bullying
while at the same time

is prepared to go
back to the same school

is puzzling
Jeremy has however

returned to school
and I hope that he carries on

as before reflecting
on the unfruitfulness

of taking
tablets

he seems to be naturally
upset about it all

he did not have psychological
disorders of any kind

which need a further
appointment here

I am therefore
closing his case

form tutor

Jeremy is
a helpful and

co-operative pupil
am I wrong

in thinking
that he has felt

considerable pressure
this year

sister

don't you
remember

they wouldn't
let us over

the white bridge
I screamed

stood up for you
they said I was

more of a man
than you'd ever be

consent

asking your mother
to agree a poem

about the one
conversation

you've ever
been able to have

mother

*all the doctors
and nurses*

*were vile
I'm sure*

*they blamed us
as if*

*I didn't feel
guilty enough*

gay men and bisexual men
are four times more likely

than heterosexual men
to attempt suicide

suicide kills more gay men
and more bisexual men than AIDS

Lifetime Prevalence of Suicide Attempts Among
Sexual Minority Adults by Study Sampling
Strategies: A Systematic Review and Meta-Analysis,
American Journal of Public Health (AJPH)

The Uncanny X-Men #134

the accepted excuse
the palatable reason why

I said I swallowed pills
was mock exam nerves

so as distraction from
impending 'O' Levels

my parents on impulse
bought me a comic

a flimsy American one
from a forecourt spindle

a first lesson in recognising
the strange fantasy of lines

how hope lies just out
of frame ready to jump

midway into a story that
if you are called names

then let them be Word
Witch or Impervious

that a hidden identity
can bestow power

over thugs and hellfire
gives you time to regroup

at a plane submerged
in the secret reservoir

ready for that final
full-page splash and

*you are no longer
the person you knew*

*you've seen flames
and life eternal*

*you are a
phoenix*

B
O
O
M
!

ode to Bronski Beat in an elevator

for Larry Steinbachek

we are all crushed together
rising through Television Centre

me twenty and dumb
them Top of the Pops

I want to confess
I've kissed a man too

New Year's Eve
four days ago

although all we did
was share a bed he said

I wasn't legal yet
but I'm petrified

someone can tell
I won't return their gaze

running
crying

I am taunting myself
making silent promises

I will not
be able to keep

praying the next floor
is where they'll get off

and when the doors ping
I finally look up

watch them strut
the fluorescent corridors

mouthing to each other
that word I cannot say

running
crying

student union disco

he would leap up to windmill
to *Blue Monday* do thigh slaps

in time only to realise too late
it was actually *Love Reaction*

by Divine the same slow build-up
that snare so similar it was hard

to tell a homage you could call it
being generous so he stops in

his tracks hesitant of the dance
like bumping into each other after

closing on College Road invited
in for tea and toast just sitting there

staring at his Lloyd Cole quiff
unsure of what music was playing

alternative night

all the men surrounding you are sweating and jumping
and dancing swerving very close and you are noticing

that they all know every word of this song and as you
watch these grinning men you are aware of warm fingers

slipping down the back of your jeans past boxer elastic
onto your skin and you're thinking perhaps some man

has pogoed sideways off their feet perhaps he's slipped
in spilt beer and grabbed the nearest thing to steady

himself which happens to be your arse but the fingers
are staying a fraction too long straying a fraction too

low for any real pretence of unintentionality and
you know you should be feeling all righteous outrage

but instead you find yourself grinning when you turn
and see this man's face so close and you both grin

both mouthing along to the words of this song
dancing a dare you never thought you'd be able

mouthing *like you*s nose to nose still standing too
close when the lights flicker on rubbing knees in the

shuffling queue to get out rushing through the precinct
finding yourself impatient for a bedsit door to unlock

on Choctaw Ridge with Spring-Heeled Jack
for Bobbie Gentry

someone will always see you
up to something

even when
you're up

to something
far away

JUMP //
DON'T JUMP //

who gives a damn
what went over that bridge

I wasn't there
I'll never say

violins mimic
a fall

you will
finish

on your

o

w

n

where trade began

this anonymous album
is a private erotic project

put together by someone attracted to
jodhpurs and guardsmen

seaports and military barracks
railway carriages

sailors town bridges
toilets taxis and public parks

gentlemen | dynion

seventeen urinals
in a row underground

you're counting them twice
while a lad notices

whistles softly
through this gift

to Cardiff men
since eighteen ninety-eight

glass bricks above
dropping light

marble wings obscure
each shuffling space

the floor is damp
slippery

you're always following
someone's shining footprints

*people living with HIV are
three times more likely than people*

*in the general population
to die by suicide*

Mortality from suicide among people living with HIV
and the general Swiss population: 1988-2017,
Journal of the International AIDS Society 22: e25339

Tabernacle Lane

a velvet staircase twists
lit by the pulse of fairy lights

the bouncer smiles
let the music decide

to dare to dance with Divine
be sure of every cheap reaction

take pride in their hand step on stage
wipe armpit sweat with a Kleenex

to hurl at the howling crowd
never apologise never hide

never let hate be unopposed
I'm that stranger desperate

for a nod a telephone number
blitzed in the dance of Saturday night

strung on barbed wire
thrown from tall buildings

for love and LUV
and X & ♥

so I asked Donna Summer and she said…

after Kim Moore

perhaps the head boy stripping
one stretch away before the high school play

perhaps the DJ snogging his hands on your hips
while his girlfriend watches from beneath neon signs

perhaps Mr Third Year saying you can sit on his knee
in a heaving Chequers then asks if you're dating Babs

perhaps Mr Letters to whom you never write back
afraid someone might read them out loud on the radio

not Mr Blind Date who's straight
and so tired of hot hot men hitting on him

not the marines and their trigger fingers
not Mr You Won't Get It From Last Dancing

not Mr Independent On The Train
not Mr Love Is Not Kind

perhaps Mr Hamlet was for real
perhaps toot toot yeah beep beep

perhaps love's about to change the past
perhaps this time your enough is enough

the Editor

for Oscar Moore

I'm listening you're talking
Hollywood premieres

sleeping off red carpets
under boardroom tables

you know so many words
it is hard to keep up

over pizza on City Road
write it all down you say

at your sister's wedding
we build people towers

you refuse to join hands
my back won't take it

I meet a man who'd worked for you
tell him how I find out

still drunk one Saturday morning
kicking a pile of *Guardians*

and your black-framed face
slides from the cover of every *Review*

you are here in a tiny book
stacked beside my bed

the spine cracked
still dazzling

heart-shaped

not jealous of your coupleness your matching
not jealous of your kitchens your itineraries

of your date nights and dramas and the back on
agains and your adopting such gorgeous acronyms

and the identical rings and the choreography
of your first dance where your mothers join in

and it took how many weeks of practice to make it
look so totally spontaneous scenes some viewers

may find distressing not jealous I could spit not
jealous I am kicking myself acting so nonchalant

aiming to be grateful for trying not to assimilate
all that's done all that will never be to create this

nightclubbing with Spring-Heeled Jack

here I am on the wrong side of a velvet rope
push past purrs Spring-Heeled Jack

here at the bar are new people to know
be a bitch grins Spring-Heeled Jack

here am I too cool to dance
quite right nods Spring-Heeled Jack

here is the man who let you in free
more drinks shrieks Spring-Heeled Jack

and here is a man who smiles
DRINK MORE! roars Spring-Heeled Jack

and I slap the base of the man's pint and
OOPS! smirks Spring-Heeled Jack

and we howl as beer splatters his face and
LEG IT! yells Spring-Heeled Jack

here is what leaps beneath my skin
here is how we terrify

Tobias and the Angel, 1989-90

for Richard Davies

struck in 1986
by the first attacks

of the HIV virus
Davies worked

more intensely
more and more

you are dead
two years before

we encounter
the Musée d'Art

Moderne de Troyes
examining your

shadowed prints of
angels and men

where the angel and
the man do not fight

I see my engravings
as poems

like a teenager
unnerved and

without language
to ask my father

secretly buys a poster
for me the angel is

towering but smiling
Tobias is lost

in the clouds
of his embrace

this has lived
with me through

every house
every mistake

I am staring
at you now

more intensely
more and more

Plasturton Gardens

in those times of lurching home far too late
you find a crop-haired young man curled tight

in the outside porch of your Pontcanna bedsit
please leave me alone I've taken some pills and

I just want to die what's the fucking point
in those years of telephone boxes you run

to dial 999 bring out a blanket to cover him with
he keeps shrugging it off starts moaning again

the ambulance crew arrive with questions slowly
coax him into their van and you go inside start

remembering those days police appear the following
morning to say he survived that it was a very near

thing puking bile across the white leather seats of our
neighbour's car who just drove and never asked why

1999 with Spring-Heeled Jack

we have always been wary of this impossible date
when it seemed such an unthinkable age to reach

so we distract ourselves and make disco buddies
with lesbians from Bristol in matching tuxedos

trading barbs with drag queens embarrassing
shirtless waiters dropping glitter into the dips

watching bespoke fireworks over Sophia Gardens
air heavy with bonfires and beacons tripping

on the balcony grazing our wrist then knowing
there's no need to join the men upstairs anymore

we don't want to fit in or impress that the answer
to our fears as the chimes begin is to dance to Prince

this one last night when it still makes sense
and babes I'm getting ready to roar

Paronella Park

José arrived from Spain alone cut cane
to buy this bend of jungle along Mena Creek

he built by hand his mortared garden
a tearoom bloomed through the pulsing green

to carry the weight of Saturday dances
red paths lined with Kauris hid water surprises

fed underground from the crooked dam
it took a decade before the jungle rebelled

swollen steel burst through plastered walls
vines crushed the roof and floods shook the rest

//

eighty years on and it's a nature reserve
I slouch at the back of the tour fall in with a man

the bus picked up last from the best hotel in Cairns
he insists on buying us both mango ice cream

he says this is his last trip back up to the North
where he was born in a shack on Magnetic Island

no water or electric just dust and tin walls
jumped a boat in the sixties got off in London

found his great love but still missed the sun
it took years of forms before they flew back together

only to nurse him alone once the virus took hold
how he would rather take pills than face that himself

tells me his life in this concrete park
falling apart in the rainforest

how deep they dive

they doze across the back seat of the bus
cupped into each other barely touching

like the sea lions a Guide had led them through
in the dawn heat of Kangaroo Island

as the bus empties they stay too close
head lying on shoulder knees nesting

a frail sanctuary from the debris and nets
the frequent collisions with pleasure boats

scarred velvet embracing as one great curve
leaving the rest of the bay deserted

to find such company after the cold waves
enjoying the warmth of a body's acceptance

a voice coming from then

the car doesn't stop
at the give way lines

heads towards my Toyota
mum is beside me

I brake hard enough to
glance rather than collide

crumpled on the same road
they'd driven me down to A&E

the closest I have been
to dying again

still upset next morning
I answer the landline

hello son it's granddad
I was worried about you both

except granddad died
two decades ago and

it's not granddad
but my uncle

although he said those precise words
and his voice was exactly the same

just one accepting adult
in a LGBTQ+ young person's life

can reduce the risk
of suicide by 40%

Accepting Adults Reduce Suicide Attempts Among
LGBTQ Youth, The Trevor Project, 2019

outside

I am licking ice cream
on a packed College Green

and this group starts chanting
I bet you love Queen

never failing to humiliate
takes me right back to being

too scared to use public transport
just walking Rufus it can start

from a car a lorry driving past
mortified by fruit and water bottles

nearly every queer person I know
has been called so many words

now when taking the train
I hide my Pride badge

if caught flaunting
I freeze

blessed vacancies

please forgive my little absences
these masterpieces dazzle me

the reflections are proving too bright
I can barely focus on the labels

please don't ask if I'm doing okay
I should have sat down let you stride ahead

but I told myself I had to keep up
so here I am trotting behind

thinking asleep but with eyelids twitching
afraid of being allowed to cross the bridge

scared of the sound of chains on the lane
outside my childhood bedroom of

knowing that behind the bricked up fireplace
they will find a young girl's remains

please forgive me I am terrified
like waking up in a hospital bed

when you think you're already home
just point me in your preferred direction

for I am anxious and angry ready to be hit
for someone to scream how they hate me

behind my counsellor's left shoulder

I see myself at eight years old
wearing the blue cardigan

mum knitted during nights
he is waving to me

from behind the tan sofa
of a room I visit every Tuesday

in a building you have to buzz
to be allowed in to

me at eight stares back
I think I'm behind a settee

watching a man watch me
he starts to cry so I cry too

only it's not our living room
and the man and the walls fade

and I'm here on top of the hayrick
staring across Back Lane

waving to Morris
returning from harvest

a pole across his shoulder
strung with twenty dead rabbits

beginners yoga with Spring-Heeled Jack

don't relax sneers Spring-Heeled Jack
this is everything we can't stand

we don't do as we are told
we won't lie down quietly

we don't care about balance
we won't recite Sanskrit out loud

and we don't sing here you ponce
a furious hiss and a jab to the ribs

from a boy you can't name
during first year assembly

see all it's brought is bad memories
and just how did Dorian Gray die

say Namaste breakdown
you think you're hilarious

sssshhh I'm the Child of Prague
one day you will chant in a temple

don't you dare try and save me
see it's released something already

the nexus of multiple realities

there is a fifteen year old you
who grows up in San Francisco

sneaks out late through a fire escape
the week following our birthday

to watch Sylvester play the
War Memorial Opera House

you join in with the slowed down gospel
chorus of *You Make Me Feel (Mighty Real)*

and your life begins in that singing
and lasts almost another nineteen years

there is a deniable you in Essex
who marries young has children

there is a you whose family moves to Edinburgh
where two days after the pills your liver fails

and the Brighton you who hates teaching
alone in a flat you can't sustain

how do you ever harmonise
how can you ever restore

so you boomerang through universes
hoping a whispered kiss will fix infinity

retired child psychiatrist

I don't think
you were mentally ill

you were just
reacting

in what you thought
was a rational way

to an intolerable
situation

at Camp Crystal Lake with Spring-Heeled Jack

hmm he says this is what happens
when you're left on your own

avoiding mealtimes
hiding in dormitories

fearing ripped men
worked up on the water

remember death doesn't scare us now
a monster is always well hidden

we are capable submerged
beneath the glimmer

the ghost of every black eye
a knife of shining bruises

I'm learning to shout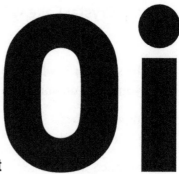

I'm learning to shout 'Oi!'
right to the back of the school bus

to all those bastards gobbing at me
every day through straws

I'm learning to shout 'Oi!'
to that car full of jocks

throwing a bucket of KFC bones
towards my fabulous friend

I'm learning to shout 'Oi!'
I am never kicking your football back

I'm learning to shout 'Oi!'
so loud your words are Jericho'd

for Travis Alabanza // for Christine Cherry

I'm learning to shout 'Oi!'
to stop you mid-pounce

'Oi!' yes we're holding hands in public
'Oi!' stay six feet away from me

'Oi!' let them
BREATHE

'Oi!' as commandment
'Oi!' as support

because who stands down
for an excuse me?

I'm learning to shout 'Oi!'
inside to myself

another Jeremy

another Jeremy

tonight I teach
another Jeremy

for the first time
say well done Jeremy

your posture is great
now loosen your spine

release those hips
hang from the waist

Jeremy stretch
relax those shoulders

lie straight both heels
touching Jeremy

69

The Proscribed Royalist, 1651
by Sir John Everett Millais

hide with me in the hollow tree
to escape whatever's approaching

outside these woods someone
is preparing to change us

a branch snaps
hooves beat

a sable paintbrush
swirls in turpentine

a bald man coughs from the hedge
of the Golf Club drive

there is a layer of terrified
beneath every moss and fern

an amplified van drives past
telling us we must stay inside

im

no release of balloons at dawn for me
no room left just as it was for me

no sewing my name on a quilt for me
no annual tears to spill for me

no keeping old shirts that smell of me
no video montages to play of me

no organising a forest search for me
no ambiguous goodbyes from me

no hideous surprise to find from me
no thinking of what to have said to me

no what ifs and could haves
as all that remains of me

never a confessional wrote by me
best to acknowledge the luck of me

accept I hold all those lost with me
those who survive left to cope are me

the Intercession

may you survive your tormentors every one
may you stand at the edge of a freshly dug pit

and scatter handfuls of joyous dirt over each taunt
may you learn of their fates while riding the X2

on the way to an emergency dental procedure and
may you ascend to that spotlit reclining chair

with a grin so wide it could snap necks
this should not feel good you are told

you are better than that
but it does and for a moment you are not

so you clap and cheer and cradle your younger self
who spends each lunchtime in an office with the head

of lower school because no system can guarantee safety
and you say to that child *I will always be here*

collecting the stains of violence the ash of each hurt
let us chant we are grateful to forgive all those words

may this vicious dust fall from our fingers and minds
may it merge with the sky of Saint Mary's Well Bay

his fire eyes flame

the ancient stones listen
I am surrounded by sheep

assertive is my favourite word
for not being ignored anymore

helping to reshape a narrative
you will do exactly as you are told

exchanging a memory of fists
for the mouth and keyboard

dear Gods don't let me become
someone who intimidates

suicide contagion
is most likely to occur

among people
who are already

depressed or
contemplating suicide

Talking About Suicide & LGBT Populations,
Gay & Lesbian Alliance Against Defamation
and Movement Advancement Project, 2011

blister packs
for S H J

pandemic paracetamol is hard
to locate during the first few weeks
mother says buy the two-pack maximum
whenever you can wherever you find them
because you won't see any if it happens again
and so now in the cupboard beneath my sink
there are packets and packets stacked on packets

fighting for space between the Vim and Domestos
there are more paracetamol tablets in my kitchen
than I ever robbed from my mother's that night
than I have ever allowed myself to own since
I consider them my isolation companions
all they ask is one kiss without foil
we are a test they whisper a test

A VOICE COMING FROM THEN

ON THIS DAY...

13 June 1231: Saint Anthony of Padua, the patron saint of lost things, dies.

13 June 1886: King Ludwig II and his physician Dr Gudden are found dead in Lake Starnberg.

13 June 1910: the moral campaigner and conservative activist Mary Whitehouse is born.

13 June 1944: six people are killed when the first V1 bomb hits London.

13 June 1964: the actor, director and playwright Kathy Burke is born.

13 June 1979: the fictional events of the film *Friday the 13th* take place (in real life it was a Wednesday).

13 June 1981: a teenager fires six blank shots at Queen Elizabeth II during Trooping the Colour.

13 June 1989: the film *Licence To Kill* is released in UK cinemas.

13 June 1994: Nicole Brown Simpson and Ronald Goldman are found murdered in Los Angeles.

13 June 1995: Alanis Morissette's third studio album *Jagged Little Pill* is released.

13 June 1997: the Oklahoma City bomber is sentenced to death.

REMEMBERING: a tiny fraction of the 800,000 people who die by suicide each year

1979 Donny Hathaway
1980 Ian Curtis
1981 Francesca Woodman
1982 Jane Arden
1983 Barney Bubbles
1984 Richard Brautigan
1985 Jeanine Deckers
1986 Richard Manuel
1987 Dalida
1988 Carter Cooper
1989 Lindsay Crosby
1990 Capucine
1991 Brad Davis
1992 Todd Armstrong
1993 Hervé Villechaize
1994 Kurt Cobain
1995 Phyllis Hyman
1996 Margaux Hemingway
1997 Billy Mackenzie
1998 Justin Fashanu
1999 Sarah Kane

2000 Richard Farnsworth
2001 Stuart Adamson
2002 Jon Lee
2003 Leslie Cheung
2004 Spalding Gray
2005 Hunter S Thompson
2006 Kuljeet Randhawa
2007 Isabella Blow
2008 David Foster Wallace
2009 Nicholas Hughes
2010 Alexander McQueen
2011 Smiley Culture
2012 Tony Scott
2013 Arpad Miklos
2014 Leelah Alcorn
2015 Lil' Chris
2016 Keith Emerson
2017 Chester Bennington
2018 Dr Julia Yasuda
2019 Keith Flint
2020 Caroline Flack
2021 —

Preventing Suicide: A Global Imperative
World Health Organization, 2014

RESOURCES

www.thecalmzone.net
*The Campaign Against
Living Miserably
(CALM) aims to prevent
male suicide in the UK.*

www.tcf.org.uk
*The Compassionate
Friends offers many
different kinds of support
for bereaved families.*

www.cruse.org.uk
*CRUSE Bereavement
Care provides support
and counselling to those
suffering from grief.*

www.ditchthelabel.org
*An international anti-
bullying charity.*

www.hafal.org
*Welsh charity for people
with serious mental
illness and their carers.*

www.listeningplace.
org.uk
*Help for those who feel
life is not worth living.*

www.maytree.org.uk
*Offers suicidal adults free
short-term stays in a safe
and caring environment.*

www.papyrus-uk.org
*Offers support and
advice to young people
at risk of suicide.*

www.samaritans.org
*Dedicated to reducing
feelings of isolation and
disconnection that can
lead to suicide.*

www.uk-sobs.org.uk
*The Survivors of
Bereavement by Suicide
(SOBS) supports all
those bereaved or affected
by suicide.*

www.TheTrevorProject.
org
*The world's largest
suicide prevention and
crisis intervention
organisation for
LGBTQ+ youth.*

NOTES

Spring-Heeled Jack is a Victorian urban legend. First sighted in 1837 he has a demonic appearance with clawed hands, fiery eyes and the ability to leap great distances and heights.

my last three months in England: the entries are from my 1977 *Puffin Readers' Diary*. All the name initials have been changed.

Trojans: the subtitle quotation is from the play *Ajax* by Sophocles.

Jeremy: the subtitle is from an article *Has there ever been a truly great man named Jeremy?* published in *The Telegraph* on 16 September 2015.

a consultant child psychiatrist's letter…: this is the text of a duplicate letter sent to my childhood GP, a copy of which I was able to read thanks to my current GP.

form tutor: an excerpt from my 1979 summer term school report.

ode to Bronski Beat in an elevator: in 1984 the age of consent for gay men in the UK was 21 years old. The photographs are of me minutes before getting in that lift.

where trade began: the poem is based on interpretation text from the exhibition *Queer British Art 1861– 1967*, which was held at Tate Britain in 2017.

the Editor: the journalist and author Oscar Moore (1960–1996) was born in London. He wrote the novel *A Matter of Life and Sex* (1991) and a regular column, *PWA (Person With AIDS)*, for *The Guardian.*

Tobias and the Angel, 1989-90: the artist Richard Davies (1945–1991) was born in Cardiff. At 15 he left home and travelled the world before settling in Paris in 1968. Quotations are based on translations from an article in issue 42 of the *Chroniques de la Bibliothèque Nationale de France.*

Paronella Park: www.paronellapark.com.au

I'm learning to shout 'Oi': this poem would not exist without me having watched Travis Alabanza's amazing performance, *Burgerz,* at the Edinburgh Fringe in 2019.

The Proscribed Royalist, 1651: was painted by Sir John Everett Millais in 1852–53. It depicts a young Puritan woman hiding a fugitive Royalist soldier in a hollow tree after the Battle of Worcester in 1651.

ACKNOWLEDGEMENTS

Many thanks are due to the editors of the following magazines where versions of these poems first appeared: Anti-Heroin Chic *(nightclubbing with Spring-Heeled Jack, beginners yoga with Spring-Heeled Jack, at Lake Crystal with Spring-Heeled Jack)*; Blog 84 *(a consultant child psychiatrist's letter…)*; Butcher's Dog *(buddies)*; Durable Goods *(on Choctaw Ridge with Spring-Heeled Jack)*; HIV Here & Now *(the Editor, Tobias and the Angel)*; Impossible Archetype *(before the motorway, the Intercession)*; Liberty Tales *(Tabernacle Lane)*; Love Bites: Fiction inspired by Pete Shelley & Buzzcocks *(alternative night);* and Places of Poetry *(gentlemen | dynion)*.

sidelines (originally titled *Arms Park*) was commended in the Café Writers Poetry Competition 2016.

Image credits: Oscar Wilde linocut (p4) © Katherine Anteney; Photographs (p8 & p36) © Ian Dixon; Collages (p8 & p36) © Jeremy Dixon; Anne Sexton Support Group badge (p11) © Hazard Press; Letterpress collages (p24 & p76) © Rachel Marsh; Collage and photographs (p50) © Janet Waters; Collage and photographs (p68) © Jeremy Dixon.

THANK YOUS

I am extremely grateful to the following people for their inspiration, guidance and support during the many and varied processes of creating this book: Katherine Anteney, Susanna Bennett, Sarah Bodman, Zoë Brigley, Angie Butler, Nancy Campbell, Susan Cousins, AR Crow, Julian Dingle, Mari Ellis Dunning, Taylor Edmonds, Conway Emmett, Marc Evans, Jamie Zoe Givens, Natalie Ann Holborow, Ian Humphries, Bernard John, Elinor Kapp, Katrina Kirkwood, Joanna Lambert, Rachel Marsh, Caleb Parkin, Cherry Potts, Grace Quantock, Shannon Ratliff, Helen Rowlands, Anna Saunders, Katherine Stansfield, Christina Thatcher, Helen Tysseling, Janet Waters and Claire Williamson.

only hindsight can write
the kindest suicide note

//

QUEER INCLUSION
IS SUICIDE PREVENTION

vOi!ce